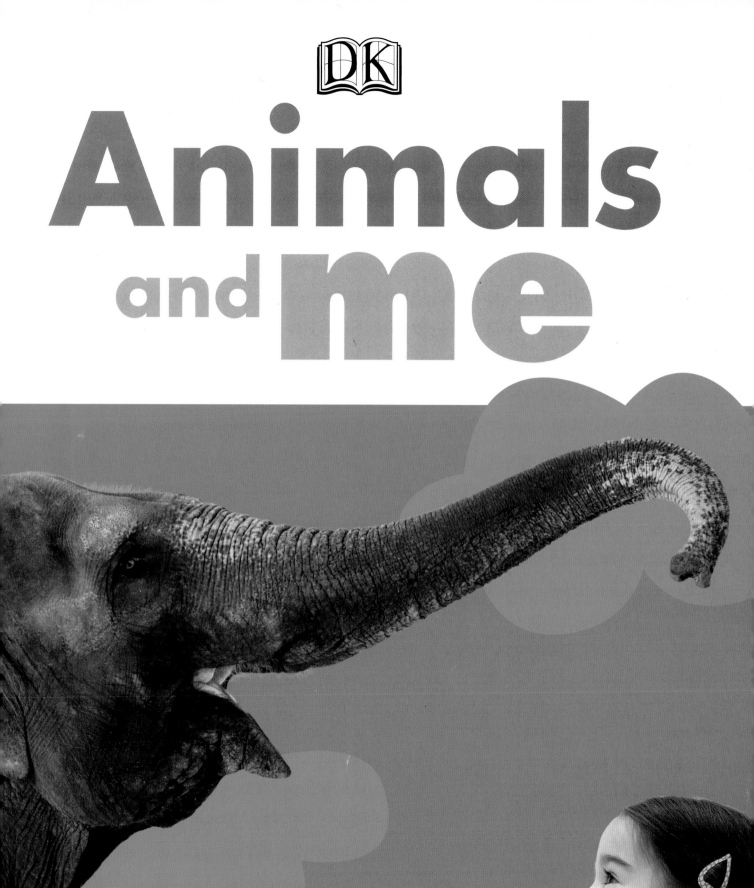

Animals and me

DK Publishing

LONDON, NEW YORK, MUNICH,
MELBOURNE, and DELHI

Written by Marie Greenwood
Designed by Victoria Harvey
Consultant David Burnie

Design development manager Helen Senior
Publishing manager Bridget Giles
Category publisher Sue Leonard
Production Rita Sinha
Production editor Siu Yin Chan
US editor Margaret Parrish
Index by Chris Bernstein

First published in the United States in 2010 by
DK Publishing
375 Hudson Street
New York, New York 10014

10 11 12 13 14 10 9 8 7 6 5 4 3 2 1

177888—05/10

A catalog record for this book
is available from the Library of Congress.

ISBN 978-0-7566-6886-0

Printed and bound in China by Toppan Printing Co. Ltd.

**Discover more at
www.dk.com**

Contents

Animal life

We are just one animal among many. As you will see on these pages, there is an amazing variety of animals living in the world today.

Animal groups

Animals that share certain features are grouped together. This helps us to understand them. The main animal groups are shown here.

My group

We belong to the group of animals called mammals. This means we belong to the same group as chimpanzees, lions, and even bats!

Horse

Mammals

Mammals are warm-blooded and feed their babies on milk. They breathe with their lungs and are furry or hairy.

Seal

Gorilla

Killer whale

Giant panda

Kingfisher

Birds

Birds have feathers and lay eggs. Most birds fly, but some of the larger birds, such as penguins, can't.

Flamingo

Owl

Penguin

Bannerfish

Goldfish

Angelfish

Snake

Butterfly

Hoverfly

Sting ray

Gecko

Dragonfly

Fish

Fish live in water. They are covered in scales and have fins. They breathe through their gills.

Archer fish

Regal tang fish

Clown fish

Reptiles and amphibians

Reptiles have dry, scaly skin and sometimes bony plates. Amphibians have thin skin and live partly in water, partly on land.

Invertebrates

Invertebrates don't have a backbone, and most are insects. There are more invertebrates than all other groups combined.

Centipede

Crocodile

Spider

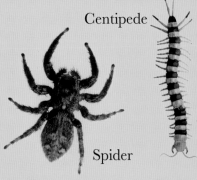

Tortoise

Octopus

Eel

Poison dart frog

Shaping up

Our skeletons give shape and strength to our bodies and protect the soft parts inside. Animals' skeletons work in much the same way, but while many are on the inside of the body, like ours, some are on the outside.

My skeleton

Your skeleton is made up of 206 bones. They are light enough so that you can move around easily. At the top of the skeleton is the skull, protecting the brain from harm.

Your spine, or backbone, is made up of lots of small bones called vertebrae. Attached to the spine is the rib cage; it protects your heart and lungs.

me!
The thighbone is the biggest bone in the body.

Animal skeletons

Animals can be split into two groups. Birds, mammals, and fish have backbones and are called vertebrates. Insects and spiders have no spines and are called invertebrates.

flutter! flutter!

Animal!
Frogs have very short spines and long legs to give them strength to jump.

A bird's skeleton is made up of light, hollow bones that allow it to fly.

meow!

A cat's skeleton is typical of other mammals, with a backbone, ribs, and skull.

Insects and spiders wear their skeletons on the outside of their bodies rather than on the inside. Their bodies are split into segments and protected by an outer casing.

A beetle's body is protected by a tough outer shell, like a suit of armor.

Wriggle! Wriggle!

A worm has no skeleton—its body is divided into muscle segments.

A fish's flexible spine allows the fish to bend its body from side to side so it can swim smoothly through the water.

Cover up

Our skin is like the body's overcoat, protecting us from injury and infection. Animals also wear all kinds of coverings, which keep them warm and safe.

In my skin

Your skin protects you from the outside world and keeps you at the right temperature. Although it looks hairless, even a newborn baby's skin is covered in millions of hairs.

ME!

The skin is the human body's largest organ.

Glub!

Fish are covered in tiny plates, called scales. They protect the fish and allow them to move freely through the water.

Anyone home?

A tortoise's hard shell protects its soft inner body, but it is heavy to carry around.

Animal!

A whale's skin can be up to 4 in (10 cm) thick.

Meow!

Cats, like many other mammals, are covered in fur, which keeps them warm and dry. They spend hours licking their fur to keep it clean.

Animal coverings

Animals may have hairy, furry, scaly, or even bristly coverings. But birds are the only animals that are covered in feathers. Feathers keep birds warm and dry and help them to fly.

A rhinoceros's tough, leather skin is like a suit of armor. It makes ideal protection, since animals have such trouble biting into it!

Some caterpillars have spiny bristles that put off other animals that might want to eat them.

Ladybugs have hard wing cases, which make it difficult for other insects to attack them.

Chomp!

stomp! *stomp!*

Elephants look flat-footed, but, in fact, they walk on tiptoe. Their toes are buried inside their feet.

Our feet and legs contain powerful muscles that help us to walk, run, jump, skip, and hop.

Feet first

While we walk upright on two feet, leaving us free to use our two hands, most mammals and reptiles walk on four feet, while insects walk on six.

My feet

Our feet are very bony. A quarter of our bones are found in our feet, and, yet, just two of these bones carry most of our weight.

Animals' feet

In addition to varying in number, animals' feet come in all shapes and sizes, especially suited to their needs—whether swimming, trotting, or hopping.

clip!

clop!

Ostriches need to run fast, because they cannot fly. They run on the bones of their toes.

Horses run on the tips of their toes on hooves, which are really just thickened nails.

A kangaroo's long toes help it to spring off the ground when hopping.

Me!
The thickest skin on your body is on the soles of your feet.

Moles use their broad, blunt front feet like shovels to dig up soil.

Boing!

A duck's webbed feet act like paddles as it swims through the water.

Animal!
A squirrel's claws are curved and pointed to dig into tree bark.

Moving on

Every time we move, we use hundreds of muscles. Animals, too, move in all kinds of ways, from slithering on land to flying in the air.

Animal moves

Whether on land or in the air, animals have to move to find food, look for a mate, and to escape from other animals that might want to eat them.

Peregrine falcons glide above their prey, waiting to pounce. When they dive, they reach speeds of 200 mph (320 km/h), faster than any other bird.

Glide!

Hum hum!

Hummingbirds can hover in the air and are the only birds that can fly backward.

The cheetah is the fastest animal on land. It can accelerate faster than a sports car!

The antelope is a shy, gentle creature whose ability to run fast helps it escape from predators.

one!

two!

three!

splash!

Frogs use their two powerful hind legs to help them to jump. They use their arms to protect them when they land.

Moles shift soil with their front feet as they burrow underground.

My moves

Your brain is in charge of your muscles, controlling every movement. It sends signals to each muscle, saying when to run and when to jump.

Me!
You use about 200 muscles every time you take a step.

Dragonflies are fantastic at flying. They can hover, fly forward and backward, and quickly change direction.

Buzz!

Flutter!

Butterflies and moths can glide as well as fly. They are the only insects that have scaly wings.

Bats are the only mammals that can fly. They also use their wings to catch insects.

A snake crawls on its ribs along the ground.

Sloths move slowly from tree branch to tree banch.

Slither!

The tortoise can only move slowly, it has such a heavy shell to carry around.

Worms move by shortening and lengthening their bodies.

Snails slide slowly along on a soft pad, called a foot.

Animal!
The Australian rocket frog can leap over 50 times its body length.

Grasshoppers are great at jumping, which makes up for their weakness at flying.

Kangaroos use their two long feet to push off from when hopping.

Boing!

Horses are strong swimmers. They paddle with their legs and enjoy being in the water.

Neigh!

Frogs use their long, powerful back legs and webbed feet to push themselves through the water.

In the swim

Unlike fish, frogs, and other sea creatures that swim instinctively and are specially adapted to living in the water, we have to be taught to swim.

Breathing in

We can only stay under water for a short time, before coming up to breathe in oxygen from the air.

Fish take in oxygen from the water through their gills.

When we swim the breaststroke, we bend our legs up, then push them out in much the same way that a frog does.

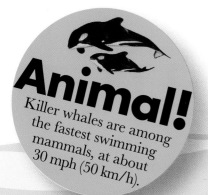

Paddle paddle...!

Swimming mammals

Many mammals not naturally adapted to living in water can swim. This includes most dogs, who even have a swimming style, the doggy paddle, named after them!

Jellyfish open and close their bodies to swim, letting the ocean's currents push them through the water.

An octopus propels itself through seas and oceans by sucking up water into its body then squirting it out.

Me!

The front crawl is the fastest swimming stroke, at about 5.3 mph (8.5 km/h).

Fish swim by bending their bodies from side to side, while steering and balancing with their fins.

Glub Glub!

Seahorses swim upright, and so only move slowly. To hide from predators, they anchor their tails in seaweeds and corals, and stay very still.

Think about it

It is our brain power above all else that sets us apart from other animals. However, many other animals show signs of intelligence that are unique to them.

My brain

Your brain is central to what makes you human. It allows you to think, reason, remember, speak, and to do everyday things.

ME!
Your brain is about the size of two fists.

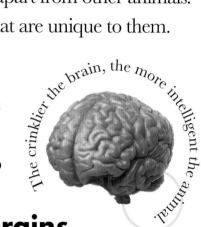

The crinklier the brain, the more intelligent the animal.

Animals' brains

Most animals have brains, but some are more highly developed than others. Aside from humans, dolphins, chimpanzees, and octopuses count among the smartest.

Elephants have great memories. They can remember where to go to find water holes, months after they've visited them.

Sheep are good at recognizing each other's faces—although they look much the same to us.

A chimpanzee's intelligence is the closest to ours. They can recognize themselves in a mirror and use simple tools.

baaa!

Animal!

The purple flatworm can find its way through a maze.

Dolphins can perform tricks, ride along by the sides of boats, and have even been used to guard ships and submarines.

splash!

Just because an animal has a larger brain, this doesn't mean it's smarter. It's how big the animal's brain is in proportion to its size that counts.

An octopus is very bright. It can tell different shapes and patterns apart. It can also solve problems, such as opening jars.

Ants are intelligent as a group. They work together to help each other across obstacles.

Some dog breeds are highly intelligent and can be trained to do various jobs. Labradors, for instance, make excellent guide dogs for the blind.

A sea lion can learn tricks, such as catching and balancing a ball on its nose.

Who's a pretty girl then..?

Parrots have an amazing ability to learn words, and some can even speak in whole sentences.

Eye see

Our eyes work with our brains, allowing us to see.
Some animals, including birds of prey, can see more clearly than we can.

My eyes

When we look at something, nerves in our eyes send messages to our brains. The brain then tells us what we've seen.

ME!
You blink at least 9,000 times a day.

Tarsiers are monkeylike animals whose eyes are bigger than their brains. Their large eyes help them to see in the dark.

A chameleon's eyes move independently, so it can see in two different directions at the same time.

Squeak!

18

Animals' eyes

Some animals depend on good eyesight in order to survive. Birds of prey need to see long distances in order to find food to eat.

A fly's large, curved eyes mean they can spot something coming from any direction. It can't see details though. To a fly, the world is made up of dots.

Buzz!

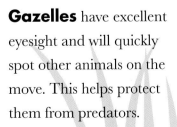

Squawk!

Many birds have eyes on both sides of their heads, so they can see all around them. Birds of prey have eyes that face partly forward, and work together to judge distances.

A mantis shrimp has the most complex eyes in the animal kingdom, allowing it to spot different types of coral or prey.

Animal!
The tuatara has three eyes—one is on top of its head.

The jumping spider has eight eyes. The biggest pair face forward and are used for pinpointing their prey.

Gazelles have excellent eyesight and will quickly spot other animals on the move. This helps protect them from predators.

squeak!

squeak!

Listen in

We use our ears to pick up sounds and to help us balance. Many animals can hear much better than we can.

Animal!

Crickets have ears on their front legs.

Animals' ears

Animals hear sounds at different frequencies, or pitches. Bats can hear very high frequencies, which the human ear can't pick up on.

Elephants have huge ears, but cannot hear any better than lots of animals. They have big ears so that they can flap them to keep cool in the heat.

Swivel!

Foxes like this fennec fox swivel their ears so they can tell where a sound is coming from.

Squeak!

A dolphin makes clicks and squeaks that bounce off things in the water and return to the dolphin's ears as echoes.

Squeak!

Bats have fantastic hearing. They use their huge ears to listen out for echoes bouncing off their prey in the dark.

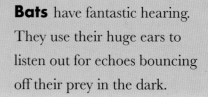

me!

Everyone's ears are a different shape.

My ears

What we call ears are just the two outer flaps that we can see. They act like funnels, collecting sounds in the air and sending them into the inner parts of the ears.

Hello! .... Hello!

Sounds are created by tiny vibrations. With this string telephone, the vibrations of your voice travel along the string from one end to the other.

Dolphins have tiny holes for ears.

Click click!

Being nosey

We breathe and smell through our noses. Some animals have a much stronger sense of smell than we do. They use their noses to sniff out food.

Whoosh!

Animals' noses

Animals can do clever things with their noses. An elephant sucks up water with its trunk for drinking and washing. An elephant's trunk is the extended part of its nose.

Animal!
A snake smells with its tongue.

An elephant also uses its trunk to pick up food, flatten trees, and roll logs.

My nose

Much of what we taste is actually what we can smell. This is because the inside of your nose is linked to your mouth, so you can smell food as you eat it.

Mmmm, smells good..!

An anteater uses its long nose to reach inside ants' nests.

A camel's nostrils are long, narrow slits. It can close them to keep sand out.

This dog has a very wet nose!

Dogs have a very powerful sense of smell. Their wet noses help them to track a scent from a long, long way away.

A pig uses its nose like a shovel to dig up bugs and snails to eat.

Sniff!

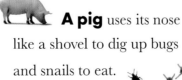

Touch it

Our sense of touch lets us know what something feels like. Animals use touch to find their way around and hunt for prey.

Animals' touch

Some animals feel things through their skin, as we do. Others touch through their hairs or whiskers, or through long pairs of sensors, called antennae.

My touch

When you touch something, tiny nerves under your skin send messages to your brain, telling you what you are feeling. Some body parts are more sensitive to touch than others.

me!
There are about 10,000 nerve sensors in your fingertips.

A walrus has a long mustache of bristly hairs that is very sensitive to touch.

Your fingertips have lots of nerves packed together, making them extra sensitive. This allows you to use light pressure when you touch delicate things, such as a butterfly.

A spider's leg is covered in hairs that pick up vibrations in the air, telling it if anything is moving close by.

A rattlesnake has two holes on its head that pick up heat given off by other animals. This helps the snake to know exactly where the animals are.

Slither... slither....!

eeek! eeek!

The two holes on a rattlesnake's head are called pits.

The tiny shrew uses its sensitive sense of touch, in addition to an excellent sense of smell and hearing, to hunt for prey.

Snap!

A lobster has two pairs of antennae, which they use to feel their way around and to find food.

meow!

meow!

A cat's whiskers are sensitive to touch and movements in the air.

Animal!
The star-nosed mole uses its 22 tentacles to sense prey.

Taste it

We use our tongues to taste all kinds of foods. Some animals have especially long tongues or extra strong jaws to help them chew their food.

My taste

Your sense of taste works closely with your sense of smell to detect different food flavors. Humans are omnivores, which means that we can eat meat, fruit, and vegetables, too.

Me!

It's thought that girls have a better sense of taste than boys.

Your tongue helps you to taste food, and to move it around in your mouth.

The chameleon sticks its long, sticky tongue out to capture insects.

Animal taste

Animals that eat meat are called carnivores. They have special tools, such as big teeth and jaws to help them chew. Animals that eat plants are called herbivores.

slurp! slurp!

Animal!

Flies taste food with their feet.

Hyenas eat meat. With their wide jaws, they can eat large animals, such as antelope.

Koalas feed on eucalyptus leaves and store them in their cheeks.

Pandas feed mainly on bamboo shoots, but also eat small animals.

Lions are big meat-eaters. They hunt most kinds of animal, including giraffes and zebras.

Giraffes are plant-eaters. A giraffe's long neck helps it reach the highest branches, and it has a long tongue to pull leaves from trees.

Hippopotamuses don't eat very much, despite their huge size. They munch on grasses in the cool of the night.

Mmm, yummy..!

Bite sized

Hamsters' front teeth keep growing all their lives.

We use our teeth to bite and chew our food, like many animals. But some animals have bigger teeth than we do, and some have no teeth at all!

Animals' teeth

Many mammals have two sets of teeth, like us. But they can look very different. Elephants have two giant teeth on each side of their mouths.

An elephant's tusks are special front teeth that grow through its lip instead of into its mouth.

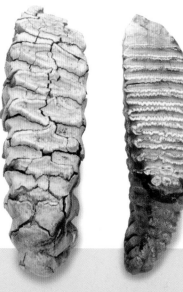

My teeth

We have two sets of teeth. The first set, called baby teeth, start to fall out when we're about six and are replaced by adult teeth. Wisdom teeth are the last adult teeth to appear.

Wisdom!

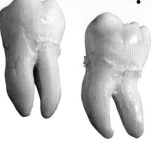

An anteater has no teeth. It doesn't need them—it just swallows insects whole.

Peck peck!

Birds are without teeth, too. They use their beaks to peck and crack open their food.

Sniff! sniff!

click!

Dolphins have lots of sharp pointed teeth— just the right shape for catching slippery fish.

Sharks have hundreds of teeth. They are replaced all the time, so they never run out, and never get blunt.

Shark attack!

Shrews have tiny, spike-shaped teeth for eating insects and worms.

Two to talk

We talk to each other using words made from sounds. But we also make signals with our hands, and make faces, too. Animals can't understand us when we talk, but they have their own kinds of sounds and signals.

Bees do a dance to tell each other where their food is.

Chimpanzees greet each other by touching hands.

Hello!

Happy talk

You don't have to make a sound to show how you feel. If the corners of your mouth turn up and your eyes twinkle, this shows you're happy!

Rabbits show a white patch under their tails or thump the ground with their hind legs when they need to warn other rabbits of danger. They even call to each other from their burrows underground.

Thump!

Birds sing for all kinds of reasons—to attract a mate, to mark where they live, to say where food can be found, and as a warning if a cat or other predator is near. Each type of bird has its own song.

Animal!

Howler monkeys are the noisiest mammals on land—they can be heard over 2 miles (3 km) away.

Swans get up close to show they like each other.

Me!

The harder I force air out of my lungs, the louder the sound!

Roar

Animal talk

Animals with bigger lungs than us, such as this tiger, make more noise. Tigers roar as a signal to other animals to keep away.

Zzzzzzzzz

Fight or flight

If threatened, animals have a variety of ways of defending themselves. Humans, too, have to decide whether to fight or take flight.

Animal defense

Animals are quick to sense danger and then to act. They may run or fly away, disguise themselves, or stand their ground and fight.

taking flight!

Ducks, like most birds, leap into the air and flap their wings to escape danger.

fooling!

A toad takes a deep breath and puffs up its body to make itself look bigger to frighten off other animals.

A hoverfly looks like a wasp and so fools predators into leaving it alone, though, in fact, it can't sting.

Puff!

fighting!

An adder sinks its poisonous fangs into an animal's skin.

My defence

If you are frightened, your body produces adrenaline, you sweat, and your heart beats faster. Adrenaline gives you energy to run away, if need be.

Run!

me!

When threatened, boys tend to fight more than girls.

Deer run quickly and dodge left and right to confuse animals that are chasing them.

A squirrel scoots up a tree trunk very fast, making it difficult to catch.

Rabbits freeze when frightened. They then run and leap in different directions.

A stick insect looks like a twig, making it hard for predators to spot.

The bittern is a wading bird that hides among tall marsh grasses.

Hide!

A tortoise pulls its soft body inside its shell when threatened.

Animal!

Earthworms can grow a new end after it's been pecked at by a bird.

The surgeonfish has sharp spines like knives on each side of its tail.

Phewy!

A skunk raises its tail and sprays a foul-smelling mist when under attack.

New life

The birth of a baby is a wonderful event. Like most mammals, we give birth to our young. Many other animals start a family by laying eggs.

me!
Humans sometimes have identical twins.

Human babies

Humans usually give birth to one baby at a time. A baby stays close to its mother for the first few years of its life.

Human babies take about a year to learn how to walk on their own.

Animal babies

Many types of animal have much bigger families than humans, and their babies often grow up faster. A baby antelope learns to walk a few hours after being born.

Sniff!

meow!

meow!

A cat recognizes her kittens by learning their smell.

Blue tits lay up to 12 eggs at one time.

A kangaroo carries her baby in her pouch. After a few months, the baby sticks its head out, before hopping out into the world.

Hello!

Glub!

Baby blue tits grow up fast. By the time they are three weeks old, they are ready to leave the nest.

Frogs lay up to 4,000 eggs. They are covered in jelly to protect the tadpoles.

Animal!

Scorpions carry their young on their backs.

Most snakes hatch from eggs. As soon as they come out, they have to fend for themselves.

Mother crocodiles can carry their babies in their toothy jaws without harming them.

Peep!

35

Family life

Many animals care for their young in groups, in much the same way as humans do. Some animal groups have several adults who share the child care.

ME!

Worldwide, more boys are born than girls.

My family

Human families vary in size. Some have one child, others have several. Children may be looked after by one or two parents, and sometimes by their grandparents, too.

Squeak! Squeak!

House mice stay close to their mothers for just three weeks.

Baby orangutans are looked after by their mothers. They stay with them until they are five or six, learning how to find food and how to make nests in trees.

Prrrrr!

Lions live together in mixed groups called prides. There are usually two to three males, up to twelve females, and lots of cubs.

Animal families

Some baby animals never see their parents, but many others stay with their parents until they are ready to look after themselves—just as humans do.

Young ostriches are protected by adult males. The strongest male looks after several families.

Baby elephants are cared for by their mothers and by their aunts.

Hello Dad!

Hello Auntie!

Prrrrr!

Prrrrr!

Growing up

We change shape as we grow, although the changes are gradual. Some animals change so much, they look completely different when older.

Me!
It's thought that we grow more quickly in the spring.

My growth
A human baby's head is quite big compared to the rest of its body, while its legs are short. As a child grows into an adult, its arms and legs grow faster than its head.

steady!

A baby harp seal feeds on its mother's extremely rich milk. This helps it triple its weight in just nine days.

Foals are the opposite of humans—they are born with long legs.

A butterfly grows through four stages as it develops. It starts life as an egg.

A caterpillar hatches from the egg. At this stage, it has no wings.

A cocoon, or chrysalis, is spun by the caterpillar. Inside, the caterpillar's body changes shape.

A butterfly eventually appears out of the cocoon. Its wings unfurl, ready to...

...fly away!

Hello!

Animal!

Baby emperor angelfish are blue and white; adults have yellow stripes.

Animal growth

Some baby animals grow and develop so that they behave differently as adults. For instance, a tadpole can only live in water, but frogs can live and breathe on land.

ribbit!

Flamingos have small, straight beaks when they hatch. In a few weeks, their beaks grow fast, until they are long and curved, like their parents'.

Frogs start life as frog spawn—a mass of eggs covered in jelly.

Tadpoles hatch from the eggs and swim with their tails.

The tadpole loses its tail and sprouts legs, eventually turning into an adult frog.

Growing older

We stop growing when we become adults and start to show signs of aging at around 40 years. However, some animals keep growing all their lives.

My aging

Although we're fully grown when we're about 20, our muscles continue to develop and our bones to harden for several more years. Signs of aging vary greatly, and many older people live full, active lives.

As people age their hair tends to turn gray and their skin becomes wrinkled.

ME! Our breastbone is the last bone to harden, when we're about 25.

Bowhead whales are the longest living mammals: some live for more than 150 years.

Giant clams, once settled in their home on the seabed, stay there for more than 100 years.

Thin on top.....

Chimpanzees can go bald as they age, just like humans!

Animals aging

The lengths of animals' lives varies—from a few days to more than 100 years. Animals in the wild don't tend to grow old and slow up like we do though—they usually remain active.

Japanese koi fish can live for around 200 years in ponds and water gardens.

A mayfly has a brief life. Once it becomes an adult, it lives for just one day.

A male orangutan shows its age by developing huge flabby cheeks and a double chin.

big...bigger..!

A male deer grows a new pair of antlers every year, and each year they get bigger.

Giant tortoises can live for much longer than us—some live for nearly 200 years.

Swifts can sleep while flying in the air.

Me!
We all dream when we're asleep, but we don't always remember our dreams.

night night!

We often sleep curled up and on our sides.

Go to sleep

Sleep is vital to life. All animals, including humans, need to sleep in order to rest their bodies and minds, save their energy, and stay healthy.

Leopards spend many hours a day resting in tree branches. They need a lot of sleep to give them energy for hunting.

ZZZzz

My sleep

When we're asleep, our heartbeat and breathing slow down and our muscles relax. We spend an average of eight hours a night asleep—that's about one-third of our lives.

Giraffes only need about two hours' sleep a night. They usually sleep standing up, like horses do.

Animals' sleep

Some mammals, including bats, hedgehogs, and mice, go into a deep sleep throughout the winter months. This is called hibernation.

Bats sleep during the day, hanging upside down. Fruit bats wrap their wings around themselves, like a blanket.

Fish don't have eyelids, so they sleep with their eyes open.

Animal!

A dolphin sleeps with just half its brain switched off—so it stays alert to danger.

Chimpanzees make nests in trees to curl up and go to sleep in.

Cats sleep a lot, but their sleep is light, and they wake up easily—a good defense against predators.

Pythons sleep for about 12 hours a day, but they can't close their eyes, since they don't have eyelids.

Koalas sleep for about 20 hours a day. They need lots of rest because their bodies take a long time to digest their food.

snore...

Record holders

Fastest, slowest, toothiest, brainiest—here are some amazing animal record breakers. Which record do we hold?

Speed

The cheetah is the fastest land animal, sprinting up to 75 mph (120 km/h).

The dragonfly is the fastest flying insect, with speeds up to 53 mph (85 km/h).

The three toed sloth is the slowest mammal, moving at 0.1 mph (0.16).

Covering

The Arctic fox has the warmest fur of any land mammal.

Size

The blue whale is the largest animal, up to 115 ft (35 m) long.

The king cobra is the longest poisonous snake, growing up to 18 ft (5.6 m).

The Atlas moth is the largest moth, at 1 ft (30 cm) across.

Intelligence

Humans are the most intelligent of all mammals.

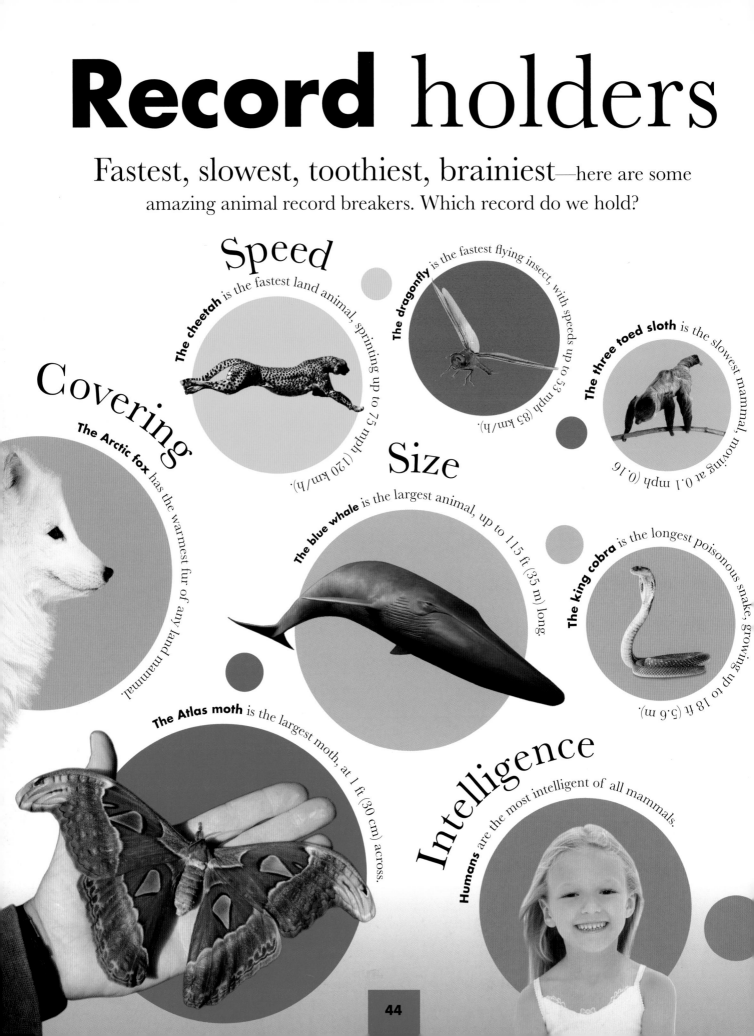

Smell

Dogs have the best sense of smell—they can smell about a million times better than we can.

Swimming

The sperm whale is the deepest diving mammal, diving up to 10,000 ft (3,000 m).

Feet

The jacana has the biggest feet in proportion to its size, at 4 in (10 cm) wide.

Taste

The giant anteater has the longest tongue of all land animals, at about 24 in (60 cm).

Teeth

Sharks have the most teeth of any animal—up to 3,000.

Life span

The giant tortoise has the longest life span, at nearly 200 years.

Eyes

The giant squid has the biggest eyes of any animal, at about 11 in (28 cm).

The octopus is the most intelligent invertebrate.

Ears

The African elephant has the biggest ears, at about 42 in (107 cm) wide.

Glossary

Adapted—especially suited to particular conditions, for example, a fish in water.

Adrenaline—a chemical produced by the body that gives you energy in moments of stress.

Amphibian—a cold-blooded animal with thin, moist skin that lives partly on land, partly in the water.

Antennae—feelers, found in some invertebrates, that help in finding food.

Breastbone—long, flat bone in the middle of the chest.

Carnivore—an animal that eats meat.

Gills—the parts of a fish that let it breathe in water.

Herbivore—an animal that eats plants and no meat.

Hibernation—to spend the winter months in a deep sleep.

Invertebrate—an animal with no backbone, for example, insects, such as butterflies.

Mammal—a warm-blooded animal that is covered in fur or hair, breathes with its lungs, and feeds its young on milk.

Nerves—strands that connect the brain to various parts of the body.

Omnivore—an animal that eats meat and vegetables.

Organ—a part of the body that has a particular job to do.

Oxygen—gas that is part of the air, which supports life.

Predator—an animal that hunts another animal in order to kill and eat it.

Prey—an animal that is, or could be, killed and eaten by another animal.

Pride—a group of lions that lives together.

Reason—to think things through in a clear and ordered way.

Reptile—a cold-blooded animal that has a dry, scaly skin, and sometimes bony plates.

Scales—small, overlapping plates that cover an animal, especially fish or reptiles.

Segments—separate parts of a jointed animal, especially insects.

Sensor—something that can detect a change in the body or the outside world.

Tadpole—a young frog or toad, before it is fully developed.

Tentacle—a long, thin, and flexible "arm" used to feel and hold things.

Vertebrate—an animal with a backbone, for example, all mammals, such as humans.

Webbed—thin pieces of skin joining the feet of an animal, especially birds.

Index

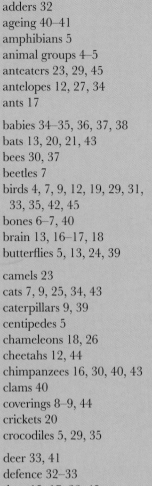

Picture Credits: Alamy Images: AfriPics.com 20fbl, 42bl; Arco Images GmbH / *Delpho, M.* 42tr; Arco Images GmbH / *Frei, H.* 14cra; Arco Images GmbH / *Reinhard, H.* 33cr; Arco Images GmbH / TUNS 9ca, 9cla, 46tr; Arco Images GmbH / *Wegner, P* 17tr; Big Pants Productions 33fbr; *Blickwinkel / Fotototo* 8cr, 8crb, 8fcr, 47cl, 47cr; *Blickwinkel / Liedtke* 3fclb; *Blickwinkel / McPhoto / PUM* 27tr; *Blickwinkel / Poelking* 29cr; *Blickwinkel / Schmidbauer* 47cla; Anna *Blume* 29tr; Penny Boyd 37r; Mike *Buxton / Papilio* 41tr; Malcolm Case-Green 15fcr; *CGElv* Austria / *Elvele* Images Ltd 28br; David Chapman 4cra; Coaster 43r; Redmond Durrell 17fcr; Chad Ehlers 41br; Bob *Elsdale* / Eureka 23fbl; Paul Fleet 15tl; Jason *Gallier* 34cra; *Clynt Garnham* 14tl; Mike *Grandmaison* / All Canada Photos 41bl; *Grant Heilman* Photography / *Runk / Schoenberger* 29cra; Alistair Heap 26cla; Dallas and John Heaton / *SCPhotos* 4bc; Mark Higgins 27cla; *D. Hurst* 30cla (flower); *ianmurray* 10bc; image100 Animals D 43cl; Ernie *Janes* 27crb, 33ca; *Milivoj Jugin* / Diomedia 19ftr; *Juniors Bildarchiv* / F145 16br; *Juniors Bildarchiv* / F191 47cra; *Juniors Bildarchiv* / F259 15tr; *Juniors Bildarchiv* / F279 32cra; *Juniors Bildarchiv* / F291 32cr, 32fcr, 33cra; *Juniors Bildarchiv* / F300 41cla; *Juniors Bildarchiv* / F323 27cra; *Juniors Bildarchiv* / R304 11fcl; *Juniors Bildarchiv RF* / F368 11cr; Erich *Kuchling / Westend* 61 GmbH 31tc; *Kuttig* - People 14br; Martin Lee / *Mediablitzimages* (UK) Limited 24fcla; *Lenscap* 29tl; Colin Leslie 33cla; Life On White 14tr, 29cla; *Oyvind Martinsen* 13fcrb; *Ivor Migdoll* / Images of Africa *Photobank* 19br; Pete Oxford / Steve Bloom Images 27bl; Andrew Paterson 31cla; Paul *Springett* 01 9tl; Gerry Pearce 11fcrb; *Photoshot* Holdings Ltd 13bc; *Pictor* International / *ImageState* 17cb; *Pölzer / F1online digitale Bildagentur GmbH* 29br; Martin Ruegner / *ImageState* 18cr; Kevin Schafer / *Danita Delimont* 18fcl; Alfred *Schauhuber / Imagebroker* 26br; Ottfried Schreiter / imagebroker 41bc; Alexander *Shalamov* 45c; *Silbernicus* 42br; *Loisjoy Thurstun* / Bubbles

Photolibrary 34bl; Ann and Steve *Toon* 11tl; Sarah *Welsted* 43tl; Wildlife GmbH 25cl, 33clb; *WorldFoto* 11bl. Corbis: Tom *Brakefield* 45cr; Michele *Constantini / PhotoAlto* 24; Digital Zoo 23fbr, 46bl; DK Limited 14bl; DLILLC 30cr; Annie Engel 1br, 23ftr; Randy *Faris* 28t; Klaus *Dietma Gabbert* / EPA 27br; Image Source 30bl; Jose Luis *Pelaez, Inc.* / Blend Images 13tc; *Frans Lemmens* 20crb; Radius Images 2br; Denis Scott 40cra; Norbert Wu / Science Faction 19cra. **Dorling Kindersley:** Booth Museum of Natural History, Brighton 7clb (green bug); Jane Bull 10tr; Jeremy Hunt - *modelmaker* 16cra, 45cl; D. Hurst / *Alamy* 3bl; Natural History Museum, London 5ftr, 6tl, 7br, 40c, 46fcrb; *Staab* Studios - *modelmakers* 5fcrb; Rollin *Verlinde* 29fbl; Weymouth Sea Life Centre 17cl; Jerry Young 5cb (crocodile), 8-9b, 41cla, 41fcla. Getty Images: Aurora / James *Balog* 23cla, 23fcra; Aurora / Michael *Winokur* 3br; Digital Vision / Indeed 47tc; Digital Vision / Martin Harvey 22clb; Digital Vision / Michael Hitoshi 6br, 21br; Digital Vision / *Natphotos* 44fcl; *Flickr* / Gail *Shotlander* 36bl; *Flickr* / www.caitlindurlak.com 31bc; Gallo Images / Danita *Delimont* 30ftl; hemis.fr / *Emmanuel Berthier* 33fcr; Nicole Hill 10cr, 36cr; Image Source 8l, 16bc, 18cl, 21clb, 33tr, 34cla; The Image Bank / *Guy Edwardes* 11cb, 12fbl; Mike Kemp 26cra, 31bl; National Geographic / Joel Sartore 8bl, 44bl; QJO Images 21ca, 21fcla; *Photodisc* / David De *Lossy* 42cra; *Photodisc* / Digital Vision. 23ftl; *Photodisc* / Don *Farrall* 13fcl, 44cra; *Photodisc* / *Keren* Su 38bl; Photographer's Choice / *Burazin* 46cl; Photographer's Choice / Christian *Aslund* 23fcrb; Photographer's Choice / Gail *Shumway* 24cr, 24fil, 48ftl, 48ftr, 48tl, 48tr; Photographer's Choice / Nancy Brown 44br; Photographer's Choice / Tom Walker 12cr; *Photolibrary* / Clive *Bromhall* 18bl; *Photolibrary* / David B *Fleetham* 44c;

Photolibrary / Mike Hill 39cb; *Photonica* / Tommy Flynn 19cb, 19crb; Radius Images 33crb; Riser / *Siri* Stafford 13ca; Robert Harding World Imagery / James Hager 9cb; *Rubberball* 33tc; Howard Shooter 23cra; *Stockbyte* / John Foxx 35tc; Stone / *Freudenthal Verhagen* 42tc; Stone / Jeffrey Coolidge 13cr; Stone / Michael *Blann* 2cr; Stone / Tim *Flach* 35tr; Taxi / Martha Lazar 23cb (dog nose); Taxi / Tony Evans / *Timelapse* Library 47bl; Tetra Images 9tr; *UpperCut* Images / Tony *Arruza* 4ca. **iStockphoto.com:** Catharina van den *Dikkenberg* 40br; *Flyfloor* 38cla; Cathy *Keifer* 26bl; *Nadezhda Kulagina* 38fcla; Lisa F. Young 40bl. **Oceanwide Images:** Gary Bell 15cb, 15fcl, 19cr, 39tr; Andy *Murch* 5cla (ray). **Photolibrary:** Animals *Animals* / Michael *Habicht* 25br; Tom *Brakefield* 44cla; Digital Zoo 1l, 22-23; Flirt Collection / Chase Swift 13cb; *Fotosearch* 45br; *Fotosearch* Value 17ftl; imagebroker.net / *Bernd Zoller* 12crb; Oxford Scientific (OSF) / *Ariadne* Van *Zandbergen* 18crb; Oxford Scientific (OSF) / *Mark MacEwen* 35b; Oxford Scientific (OSF) / *Thomas Haider* 45tc; Peter Arnold Images / Gerard *Lacz* 12cb; Picture Press / Gisela *Delpho* 12c; *WaterFrame* - Underwater Images / *Reinhard Dirscherl* 45clb. **Photoshot:** NHPA / A.N.T. Photo Library 13fbl; NHPA / Charles Hood / Oceans Image 15ca, 15cra; NHPA / John Shaw 19clb; NHPA / Mark Bowler 31tr; NHPA / Martin Harvey 36br, 36-37; NHPA / Martin *Zwick* 13fbr; *Woodfall* Wild Images / Joe McDonald 37cl. **Warren Photographic:** 16cb, 17bl, 18br, 34bl; Jane Burton 7c.

Jacket images: Front: Corbis: DLILLC t. Back: **Alamy Images:** Kevin Schafer *cla.* **Getty Images:** Brand X Pictures / *Elyse Lewin fcl*; DK Stock / Robert Glenn cl.

All other images © Dorling Kindersley
For further information see: www.dkimages.com